Danish Floral Charted Designs

Gerda Bengtsson

Dover Publications, Inc.
New York

Published in Canada by General Publishing Company, Ltd., 30 Lesmill Road, Don Mills, Toronto, Ontario.
Published in the United Kingdom by Constable and Company, Ltd.

Danish Floral Charted Designs, first published in 1980, contains the charted designs originally published in Parts 1 and 2 of *Danish Embroidery,* prepared by Selskabet Til Haandarbejdets Fremme, in 1959. (Parts 3 and 4 were published under the title *Danish Pulled Thread,* Dover 0-486-23474-6.) It is reprinted by special arrangement with the original English publisher, B. T. Batsford, Ltd., 4 Fitzhardinge Street, London W1H 0AH, England. A Publisher's Note has been especially prepared for this edition.

International Standard Book Number: 0-486-23957-8

Manufactured in the United States of America
Dover Publications, Inc.
180 Varick Street
New York, N.Y. 10014

Publisher's Note

The Danish society Haandarbejdets Fremme, known abroad as Danish Design, was started in 1928 with the object of protecting and reviving embroidery, hand-weaving and home industries in Denmark. For many years the society, which is under the patronage of Her Majesty the Queen of Denmark, has published instructive books on the traditional art of Danish embroidery. This collection of floral designs by Gerda Bengtsson has been compiled from one of those books which was originally published in Great Britain in the hopes of arousing the interest of foreign needleworkers to the great traditions of Danish cross-stitch.

Although charted designs can be used in many different forms of needlework, such as needlepoint, latch-hooking, crocheting and knitting, these designs were originally created for counted cross-stitch. Counted cross-stitch is very simple. The basic ingredients are a small, blunt needle and a fabric that is woven so evenly it appears to be formed in regular blocks or squares. Push the threaded needle up through a hole in the fabric and cross over the thread intersection (or square) diagonally, left to right (*diagram 1*). This is half the stitch. Now cross back, right to left, making an X.

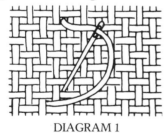

DIAGRAM 1

Counted cross-stitch is an ancient skill that has been practiced and perfected with slight variations in technique all over the world. Here in America and in the Scandinavian countries, the bottom stitches traditionally slant left to right and the top stitches right to left. In England, however, the stitches slant in the opposite directions. It really makes no difference which technique you adopt *as long as you are consistent* throughout your piece of work.

In America an embroidery hoop is used, and the work is done with the stab stitch, in which one comes up through a hole on one journey and then goes down through the next hole in a separate journey. In many other parts of the world, however, cross-stitchers use a continuous sewing-stitch motion, and the work is done without a hoop.

One of the great advantages to counted cross-stitch is that the supplies and equipment required are minimal and inexpensive. You will need:

1. A small blunt tapestry needle, #24 or #26.
2. Evenweave fabric. This can be linen, cotton, wool or a blend that includes miracle fabrics. The three most popular fabrics are:

Cotton Aida. This is made 14 threads per inch, 11 threads per inch, 8 threads per inch, and so forth. Fourteen, being the prettiest, is preferred.

Evenweave Linen. This also comes in a variety of threads per inch. Working on evenweave linen involves a slightly different technique, which is explained on page iv. Thirty-count linen will give a stitch approximately the same size as 14-count aida.

Hardanger Cloth. This has 22 threads per inch and is available in cotton or linen.

3. Embroidery thread. This can be six-strand mercerized cotton floss (DMC, Coats and Clark, Lily, Anchor, etc.), crewel wool, Danish Flower Thread, silken and metal threads or perle cotton. Danish Flower Thread and DMC embroidery thread have been used to color-code the patterns in this book. For 14-count aida and 30-count linen, divide six-strand cotton floss and work with only two strands. For more texture, use more thread. Crewel wool is pretty on an evenweave wool fabric. Danish Flower Thread is a thicker thread with a matt finish, one strand equalling two of cotton floss.

4. Embroidery hoop. Use a plastic or wooden 4", 5" or 6" round or oval hoop with a screw type tension adjuster.

5. A pair of sharp embroidery scissors are absolutely essential.

Prepare the fabric by whipping, hemming, or zigzagging on the sewing machine to prevent ravelling at the edges. Locate the exact center of the design you have chosen, so that you can then center the design on the piece of fabric. Next, find the center of the fabric by folding it in half both vertically and horizontally. The center stitch of the design should fall where the creases in the fabric meet.

It's usually not very convenient to begin work with the center stitch itself. As a rule it's better to start at the top of a design working horizontal rows of a single color, left to right. This technique permits you to go from an unoccupied space to an occupied space (from an empty hole to a filled one), which makes ruffling the floss less likely. To find out where the top of the design should be placed, count squares up from the center of the design, and then count off the corresponding number of holes up from the center of the fabric.

Next, place the section of the fabric to be worked taughtly in the hoop; the tighter the better, for tension makes it easier to push the needle through the holes without piercing the fabric. As you work, use the screw adjuster to tighten as necessary. Keep the screw at the top and out of your way. When beginning, fasten the thread with a waste knot by holding a bit of thread on the underside of the work and anchoring it with the first few stitches (*diagram 2*). Do all the stitches in the same color in the same row, working left to right and slanting from bottom left to upper right (*diagram 3*). Then cross back, completing the X's (*diagram 4*). Some cross-stitchers prefer to cross each stitch as they come to it; this is fine, but be sure the slant is always in the correct direction. Of course, isolated stitches must be crossed as you work them. Vertical stitches are crossed as shown in diagram 5. Holes are used more than once; all stitches "hold hands" unless a space is indicated. The work is always held upright, never turned as for some needlepoint stitches.

DIAGRAM 2
Reverse side of work

DIAGRAM 3

DIAGRAM 4

DIAGRAM 5

When carrying a color from one area to another, wiggle your needle under existing stitches on the underside. Do not carry a color across an open expanse of fabric for more than a few stitches as the thread will be visible from the front. Remember, in counted cross-stitch you do not work the background.

To end a color, weave in and out of the underside of the stitches, perhaps making a scallop stitch or two for extra security (*diagram 6*). Whenever possible end in the direction in which you are traveling, jumping up a row, if necessary (*diagram 7*). This prevents holes caused by work being pulled in two directions. Do not make knots; knots make bumps. Cut off the ends of the threads; do not leave any tails because they'll show through when the work is mounted.

The only other stitch used in counted cross-stitch is the backstitch. This is worked from hole to hole and may be vertical, horizontal or slanted (*diagram 8*).

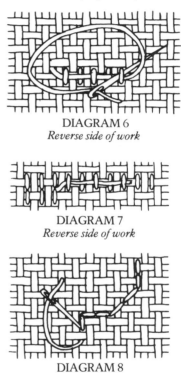

DIAGRAM 6
Reverse side of work

DIAGRAM 7
Reverse side of work

DIAGRAM 8

Working on linen requires a slightly different technique. Evenweave linen is remarkably regular, but there are always some thin threads and some that are nubbier or fatter than others. To even these out and to make a stitch that is easy to see, the cross-stitch is worked over two threads each way. The "square" you are covering is thus four threads (*diagram 9*). The first few stitches on linen are sometimes difficult, but one quickly begins "to see in two's." After the third stitch, a pattern is established, and should you inadvertently cross over three threads instead of four, the difference in slant will make it immediately apparent that you have erred.

Linen evenweave fabric should be worked with the selvage at the side, not at the top and bottom.

Because you go over more threads, linen affords more variations in stitches. A half cross-stitch can slant in either direc-

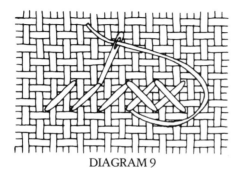

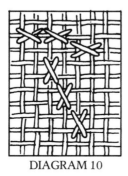

DIAGRAM 9

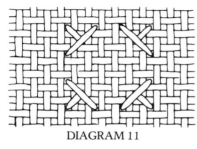

DIAGRAM 10

DIAGRAM 11

worked on a 14-count cloth, divide 112 stitches by 14 to get 8 and 140 by 14 to get 10; so the worked design will measure 8″ x 10″. The same design worked on 22-count fabric would measure approximately 5″ x 6½″.

Gingham or other checkered material can also be used for counted cross-stitch by making the crosses over the checks from corner to corner. If you wish to embroider a cross-stitch design onto a fabric which does not have an evenweave, baste a lightweight Penelope canvas to the fabric. The design can then be worked from the chart by making crosses over the double mesh of the canvas, being careful not to catch the threads of the canvas in the sewing. When the design is completed, the basting stitches are removed, and the horizontal and then the vertical threads of the canvas are removed, one strand at a time, with a tweezers. The cross-stitch design will remain on the fabric.

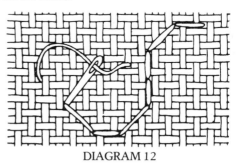

DIAGRAM 12

DIAGRAM 13

tion. Diagram 10 shows half cross-stitches worked over one thread in the one direction. A three-quarter cross-stitch is shown in diagram 11. Diagram 12 shows backstitch on linen. Diagram 13 shows four backstitches worked over a single thread and a single thread crossing. A number of the charts in this book were designed specifically for work on linen and call for the use of half cross-stitches and three-quarter cross-stitches. These stitches will have to be worked *between* holes, rather than from hole to hole, when adapted for Aida or Hardanger cloth.

Bear in mind that the finished piece of needlework will not be the same size as the charted design unless you happen to be working on fabric that has the same number of threads per inch as the chart has squares per inch. To determine how large a finished design will be, divide the number of stitches in the design by the thread-count of the fabric. For example, if a design that is 112 stitches wide by 140 stitches deep is

After you have completed your embroidery, wash it in cool or lukewarm water with a mild soap. Rinse well. Do not wring. Roll in a towel to remove excess moisture. Immediately iron on a padded surface with the embroidery face down. Be sure the embroidery is completely dry before attempting to mount.

To mount as a picture, center the embroidery over a pure white, rag-content mat board. Turn margins over to the back evenly. Lace the margins with button thread, top to bottom, side to side. The fabric should be tight and even, with a little tension. Never use glue for mounting. Counted cross-stitch on cotton or linen may be framed under glass. Wool needs to breathe and should not be framed under glass unless breathing space is left.

Your local needlework shop or department where you buy your materials will be happy to help you with any problems.

DANDELION

DMC		DANISH	
912	⊠	8	Dark Verdigris Green
320	⊠	10	Fresh Green
3348	⊡	223	Dull Light Green
444	⊕	48	Yellow
356	⊎	13	Brick Red
318	⊟	19	Light Grey
	⊡	0	White

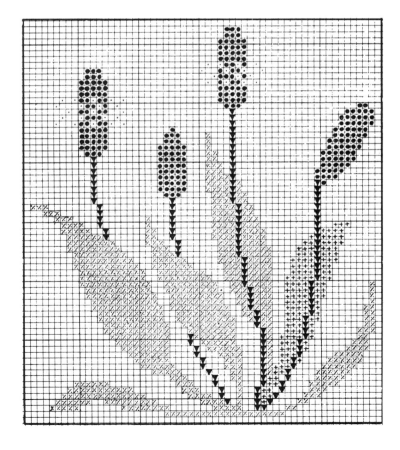

NARROW-LEAVED PLANTAIN

DMC		DANISH	
501	⊙	9	Dull Blue Green
3348	⊡	223	Dull Light Green
368	⊞	224	Verdigris Green
355	▼	214	Brownish Red
	⊡	0	White

BUTTERCUPS

DMC		DANISH	
741	◩	53	Orange Yellow
444	④	48	Yellow
368	⊞	224	Verdigris Green
3348	⊠	223	Dull Light Green
3348	⌐	223	Dull Light Green; backstitch
320	⊠	10	Fresh Green
501	◖	9	Dull Blue Green

DAISY

DMC		DANISH	
320	⊠	10	Fresh Green
3348	⊠	223	Dull Light Green
912	⊠	8	Dark Verdigris Green
444	④	48	Yellow
	⊡	0	White
3354	◩	69	Light Red
892	▣	86	Fresh Red
356	◡	13	Brick Red

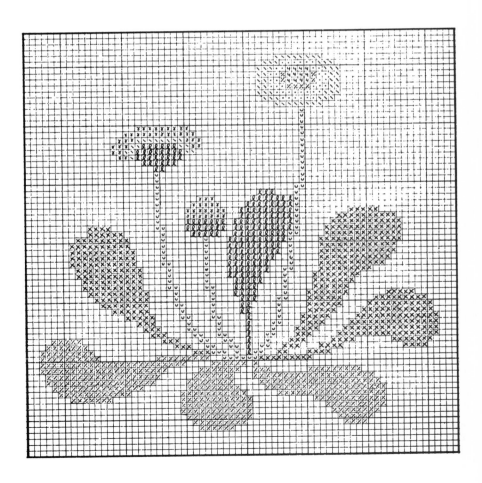

ANEMONE

DMC		DANISH	
320	⊠	10	Fresh Green
987	◖	100	Medium Green
986	◔	30	Dark Green
500	▣	210	Very Dark Green
778	⊡	1	Pale Rose
3354	◁	3	Old Rose
355	▼	214	Brownish Rose
315	▲	4	Wine Red
3021	▲	216	Very Dark Brown
640	⊞	215	Earth Color
833	③	203	Golden Yellow
833	⋯	203	Golden Yellow; backstitch
	⊡	0	White
407	⊞	15	Greyish Red
444	④	48	Yellow
3023	⌐	7	Sand Color; backstitch

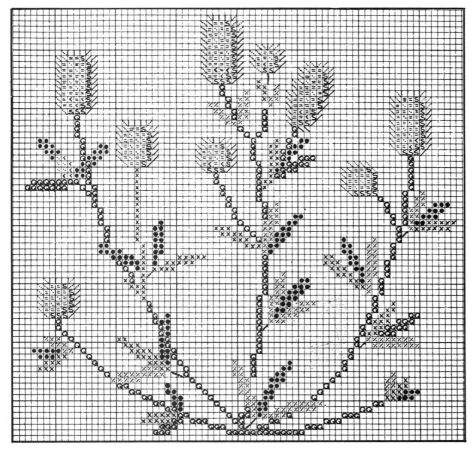

HARE'S-FOOT CLOVER

DMC		DANISH	
414	⑤	20	Grey
318	⊟	19	Light Grey
3354	◁	3	Old Rose
3354	╱	3	Old Rose; backstitch
778	⊡	1	Pale Rose
778	⋰	1	Pale Rose; backstitch
987	◖	100	Medium Green
987	⌇	100	Medium Green; backstitch
320	⊠	10	Fresh Green
320	⚡	10	Fresh Green; backstitch
501	◉	9	Dull Blue Green
3348	⬚	223	Dull Light Green

SLOES

DMC		DANISH	
3021	▲	216	Very Dark Brown
3021	◪	216	Very Dark Brown; half cross-stitch
3021	/	216	Very Dark Brown; backstitch
987	◨	100	Medium Green
987	✗	100	Medium Green; backstitch
734	◳	26	Yellow Green
734	⦂	26	Yellow Green; backstitch
833	③	203	Golden Yellow
833	⌇	203	Golden Yellow; backstitch
823	◪	201	Dark Blue
550	⊠	23	Lavender
414	⑤	20	Grey

GOOSEBERRIES

DMC		DANISH	
320	⊠	10	Fresh Green
3348	⊡	223	Dull Light Green
500	◨	210	Very Dark Green
500	≸	210	Very Dark Green; backstitch
987	◨	100	Medium Green
987	⌐	100	Medium Green; backstitch
501	◉	9	Dull Blue Green
501	⌐	9	Dull Blue Green; backstitch
677	⊟	225	Light Yellow Green
734	◳	26	Yellow Green
730	◪	34	Dark Yellow Green
730	⋰	34	Dark Yellow Green; backstitch
640	⊞	215	Earth Color
640	⦀	215	Earth Color; backstitch
3021	▲	216	Very Dark Brown
3021	◥	216	Very Dark Brown; backstitch

RED CURRANTS

DMC		DANISH	
501	◉	9	Dull Blue Green
3348	☑	223	Dull Light Green
500	◼	210	Very Dark Green
892	⊠	86	Fresh Red
831	◎	6	Dark Greenish Gold
760	◐	2	Pale Bluish Red
321	▤	97	Bright Red
640	Ⓗ	215	Earth Color
987	Ⓠ	100	Medium Green
987	〰	100	Medium Green; backstitch
320	⊠	10	Fresh Green
320	╲	10	Fresh Green; backstitch
3021	▲	216	Very Dark Brown
3021	◢	216	Very Dark Brown; half cross-stitch
3013	⬚	218	Greyish Yellow
3354	◩	69	Light Red
444	�4	48	Yellow

BLACK CURRANTS

DMC		DANISH	
320	⊠	10	Fresh Green
987	Ⓠ	100	Medium Green
3348	☑	223	Dull Light Green
500	◼	210	Very Dark Green
501	◉	9	Dull Blue Green
501	╲	9	Dull Blue Green; backstitch
550	⊠	23	Lavender
823	◪	201	Dark Blue
315	◍	94	Dark Blue Violet
3042	◿	27	Light Mauve
640	Ⓗ	215	Earth Color
436	☑	213	Medium Brown
833	⬚	203	Golden Yellow
3013	③	218	Greyish Yellow

SYCAMORE

DMC		DANISH	
320	⊠	10	Fresh Green
987	▣	100	Medium Green
987	╱	100	Medium Green; backstitch
3348	▨	223	Dull Light Green
501	◖	9	Dull Blue Green
500	◼	210	Very Dark Green
991	◪	211	Dark Blue Green
3051	✔	212	Olive Green
734	◨	26	Yellow Green
677	⊟	225	Light Yellow Green
833	▣	203	Golden Yellow
640	▥	215	Earth Color
3021	▲	216	Very Dark Brown

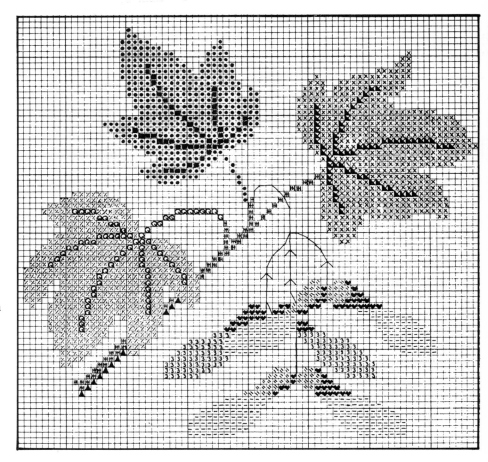

BAY-WILLOW

DMC		DANISH	
987	▣	100	Medium Green
987	⌇	100	Medium Green; backstitch
3348	▨	223	Dull Light Green
3348	⸜	223	Dull Light Green; backstitch
500	◼	210	Very Dark Green
501	◖	9	Dull Blue Green
501	⸝	9	Dull Blue Green; backstitch
320	⊠	10	Fresh Green
3347	◖	40	Fresh Pale Green
3347	╲	40	Fresh Pale Green; backstitch
734	◨	26	Yellow Green
640	▥	215	Earth Color
677	⋰	225	Light Yellow Green; backstitch

ICELAND POPPY

DMC		DANISH	
445	☑	31	Lemon Yellow
734	▨	26	Yellow Green
833	③	203	Golden Yellow
640	⊞	215	Earth Color
3348	⊠	223	Dull Light Green
991	◪	211	Dark Blue Green
368	⊞	224	Verdigris Green
935	◨	206	Dark Olive Green
935	⌇	206	Dark Olive Green; backstitch
966	◫	99	Pale Verdigris Green
730	◩	34	Dark Yellow Green
912	◐	8	Dark Verdigris Green

SNOW GENTIAN

DMC		DANISH	
3347	◁	40	Fresh Pale Green
320	⊠	10	Fresh Green
987	◙	100	Medium Green
797	◐	17	Dark Cornflower
	⊡	0	White
407	⊞	15	Greyish Red
833	③	203	Golden Yellow
355	◪	214	Brownish Red
355	◧	214	Brownish Red; half cross-stitch
322	⊞	22	Light Cornflower
322	⁛	22	Light Cornflower; backstitch
986	◪	30	Dark Green
986	⌇	30	Dark Green; backstitch
734	▨	26	Yellow Green
730	◩	34	Dark Yellow Green

MOUNTAIN
LADY'S MANTLE

DMC		DANISH	
445	◪	31	Lemon Yellow
966	▣	99	Pale Verdigris Green
3348	◪	223	Dull Light Green
987	◙	100	Medium Green
640	⊞	215	Earth Color
407	⊞	15	Greyish Red
320	⊠	10	Fresh Green
320	〜	10	Fresh Green; backstitch
734	◨	26	Yellow Green
734	⋰	26	Yellow Green; backstitch
3347	⊏	40	Fresh Pale Green
986	◈	30	Dark Green

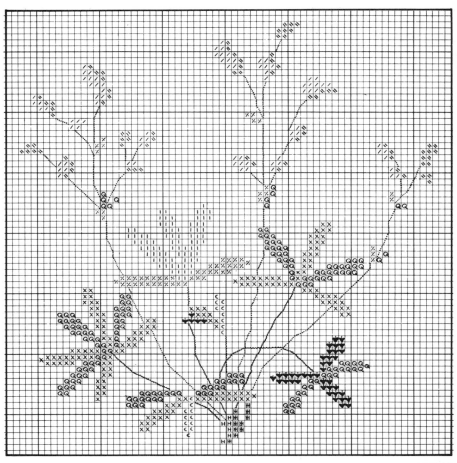

LAPLAND
RHODODENDRON

DMC		DANISH	
3354	⊏	3	Old Rose
961	◙	37	Fresh Bluish Red
309	Ⓜ	88	Bluish Red
3348	◪	223	Dull Light Green
734	◨	26	Yellow Green
991	◪	211	Dark Blue Green
987	◙	100	Medium Green
987	⌐	100	Medium Green; backstitch
730	⊠	34	Dark Yellow Green
730	〜	34	Dark Yellow Green; backstitch
730	⊠	34	Dark Yellow Green; half cross-stitch
640	⊞	215	Earth Color
3021	▲	216	Very Dark Brown
3013	⊡	218	Greyish Yellow

OPEN WINTERGREEN

DMC		DANISH	
407	H	15	Greyish Red
355	V	214	Brownish Red
320	X	10	Fresh Green
320	L	10	Fresh Green; backstitch
320	X	10	Fresh Green; half cross-stitch
778	⊡	1	Pale Rose
3348	Z	223	Dull Light Green
3348	Z	223	Dull Light Green; half cross-stitch
987	Q	100	Medium Green
961	O	37	Fresh Bluish Red
961	⌇	37	Fresh Bluish Red; backstitch
3354	<	3	Old Rose
833	③	203	Golden Yellow
986	⬛	30	Dark Green
436	Z	213	Medium Brown

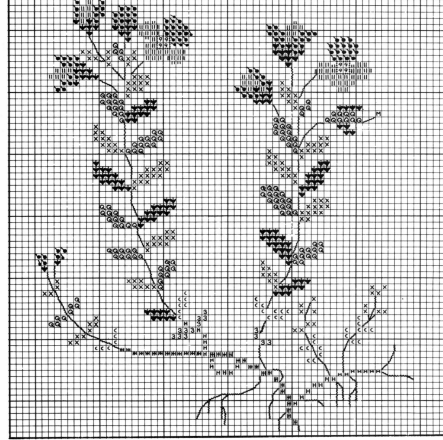

ROCK SPEEDWELL

DMC		DANISH	
833	③	203	Golden Yellow
3347	C	40	Fresh Pale Green
320	X	10	Fresh Green
986	⬛	30	Dark Green
3023	⑨	7	Sand Color
987	Q	100	Medium Green
407	H	15	Greyish Red
407	⌇	15	Greyish Red; backstitch
309	M	88	Bluish Red
309	⋰	88	Bluish Red; backstitch
797	◪	17	Dark Cornflower
797	◨	17	Dark Cornflower; half cross-stitch
322	Ⅲ	22	Light Cornflower
322	⊞	22	Light Cornflower; half cross-stitch
640	H	215	Earth Color

10

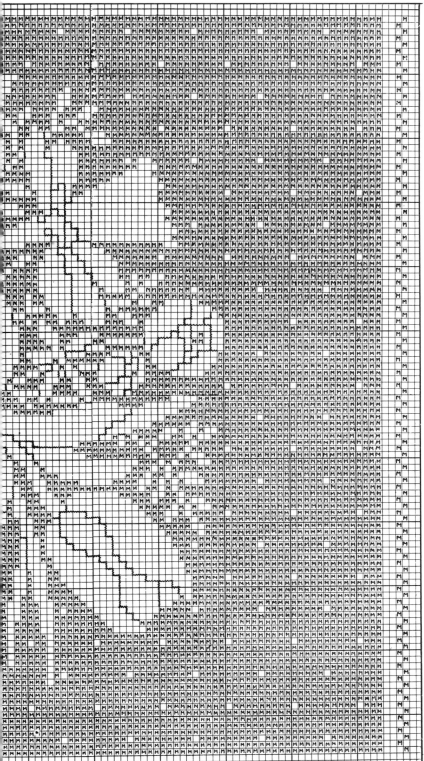

SPRING FLOWERS

DMC		DANISH	
309	M	88	Bluish Red
309	⌇	88	Bluish Red; backstitch

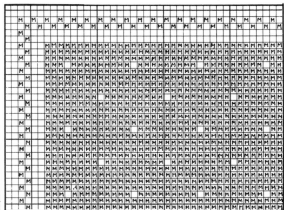

NOTE: On the chart the center is indicated by the letter ''A''. For reasons of space the design has only been drawn full width but not full height. When all of the stitches shown on the chart have been worked, continue working 26 rows of background color above and 26 below, remembering to leave space for the dots, which should be the same distance from each other as in the rest of the background. A chart for one corner is shown.

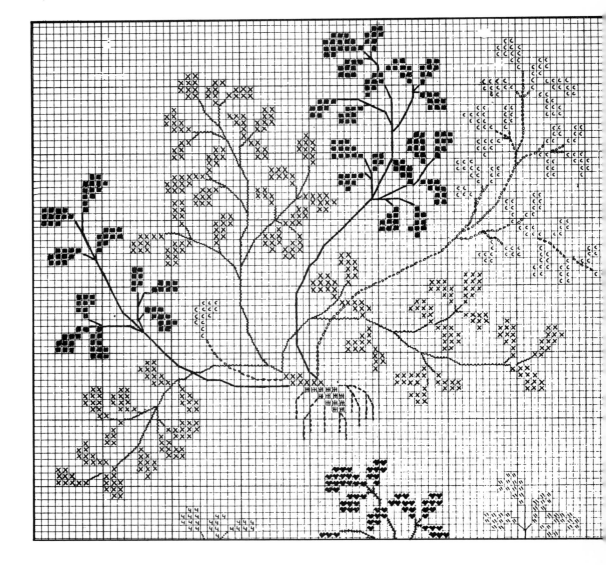

WALL-RUE REPEAT PATTERN

DMC		DANISH				DANISH	
320	⊠	10	Fresh Green	444	④	48	Yellow
320	〰	10	Fresh Green; backstitch	444	⋰	48	Yellow; backstitch
500	■	210	Very Dark Green	730	⑧	34	Dark Yellow Green
500	⌐	210	Very Dark Green; backstitch	730	✎	34	Dark Yellow Green; backstitch
3347	ⓒ	40	Fresh Pale Green	734	⑤	26	Yellow Green
3347	°	40	Fresh Pale Green; backstitch	734	⌐	26	Yellow Green; backstitch
640	⊞	215	Earth Color	3051	◙	212	Olive Green
640	¦	215	Earth Color; backstitch	3051	⚞	212	Olive Green; backstitch

NOTE: The backstitch is worked in the same color as the leaves.

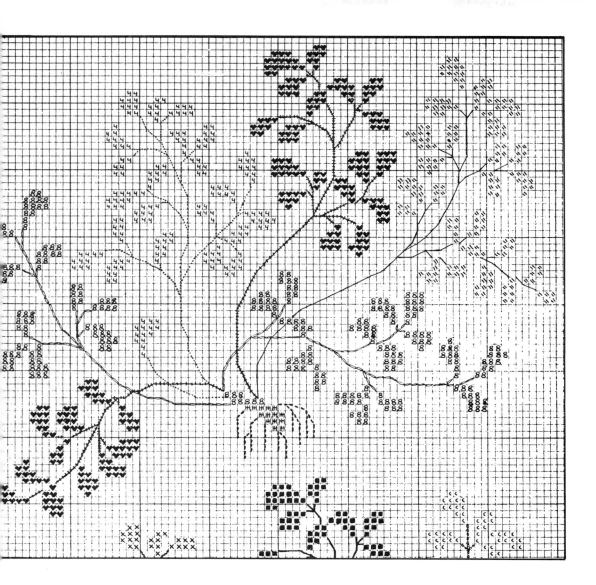

RED DEAD-NETTLE

DMC		DANISH	
961	⊙	37	Fresh Bluish Red
309	Ⓜ	88	Bluish Red
315	Ⓐ	4	Wine Red
730	◩	34	Dark Yellow Green
315	◣	29	Dark Brownish Red
3051	◪	212	Olive Green
986	◪	30	Dark Green
734	◩	26	Yellow Green
734	◲	26	Yellow Green; half cross-stitch
407	Ⓗ	15	Greyish Red
407	◰	15	Greyish Red; half cross-stitch
407	⌇	15	Greyish Red; backstitch
987	◙	100	Medium Green
3348	◪	223	Dull Light Green
3348	◪	223	Dull Light Green; half cross-stitch

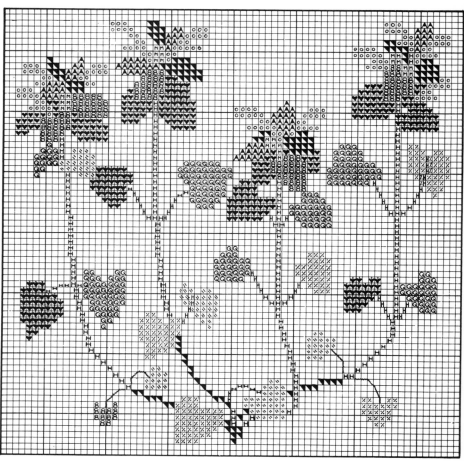

COMMON MILKWORT

DMC		DANISH	
3042	◮	27	Light Mauve
3347	◙	40	Fresh Pale Green
501	◑	9	Dull Blue Green
550	⊠	23	Lavender
320	⊠	10	Fresh Green
320	⌐	10	Fresh Green; backstitch
793	Ⓣ	21	Light Blue
793	◱	21	Light Blue; half cross-stitch
987	◙	100	Medium Green
987	◙	100	Medium Green; half cross-stitch
322	Ⅲ	22	Light Cornflower
322	◫	22	Light Cornflower; half cross-stitch

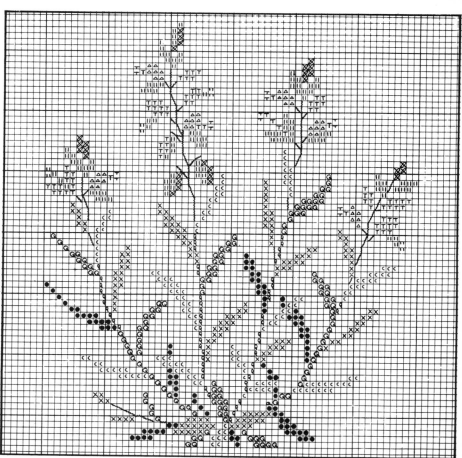

COMMON STORK'S-BILL

DMC		DANISH	
501	◓	9	Dull Blue Green
3348	▨	223	Dull Light Green
987	◕	100	Medium Green
355	▼	214	Brownish Red
355	◤	214	Brownish Red; half cross-stitch
961	◯	37	Fresh Bluish Red
961	◖	37	Fresh Bluish Red; half cross-stitch
407	⊞	15	Greyish Red
407	⋰	15	Greyish Red; backstitch
730	⑤	34	Dark Yellow Green
730	⌐	34	Dark Yellow Green; backstitch
833	③	203	Golden Yellow
833	⊠	203	Golden Yellow; three-quarter cross-stitch
320	⊠	10	Fresh Green
320	◪	10	Fresh Green; three-quarter cross-stitch

LAMB'S TONGUE PLANTAIN

DMC		DANISH	
778	⊡	1	Pale Rose
3013	⊡	218	Greyish Yellow
3348	▨	223	Dull Light Green
935	◑	206	Dark Olive Green
986	▲	30	Dark Green
987	◕	100	Medium Green
320	⊠	10	Fresh Green
3347	◁	40	Fresh Pale Green
356	↘	13	Brick Red; backstitch

HOP-MEDIC

DMC		DANISH	
966	⊡	99	Pale Verdigris Green
445	◪	31	Lemon Yellow
501	◖	9	Dull Blue Green
501	◖	9	Dull Blue Green; half cross-stitch
501	❟	9	Dull Blue Green; backstitch
320	⊠	10	Fresh Green
320	⫽	10	Fresh Green; backstitch
3347	ᴄ	40	Fresh Pale Green
3347	⁄	40	Fresh Pale Green; backstitch
987	◨	100	Medium Green
987	⌇	100	Medium Green; backstitch
3348	⊡	223	Dull Light Green
3348	◪	223	Dull Light Green; half cross-stitch
3348	⠄⁄	223	Dull Light Green; backstitch

SWEET VIOLET

DMC		DANISH	
741	◙	53	Orange Yellow
327	▣	5	Lilac
3042	△	27	Light Mauve
320	⊠	10	Fresh Green
987	◨	100	Medium Green
986	◙	30	Dark Green
407	⊞	15	Greyish Red
3348	◪	223	Dull Light Green
3348	⠛	223	Dull Light Green; backstitch

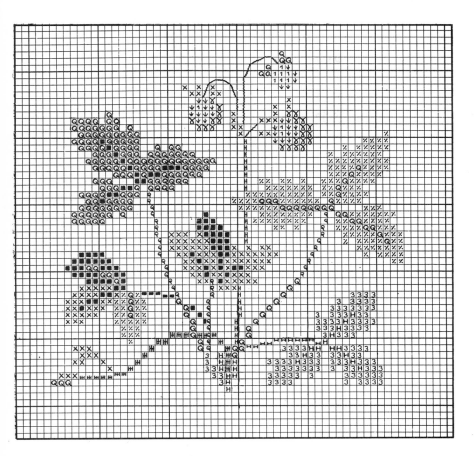

WOOD STRAWBERRY

DMC		DANISH	
320	⊠	10	Fresh Green
892	⊠	86	Fresh Red
921	↓	95	Carrot Color
950	1	25	Flesh Color
833	③	203	Golden Yellow
987	ⓠ	100	Medium Green
987	ⓠ	100	Medium Green; half cross-stitch
987	⌐	100	Medium Green; backstitch
3348	⊡	223	Dull Light Green
500	■	210	Deep Dark Green
500	⌐	210	Deep Dark Green; half cross-stitch
640	⊞	215	Earth Color
640	⊡	215	Earth Color; half cross-stitch
407	⊞	15	Greyish Red
407	⊞	15	Greyish Red; half cross-stitch

STONE BRAMBLE

DMC		DANISH	
353	⊡	12	Light Brick Red
987	ⓠ	100	Medium Green
3348	⊡	223	Dull Light Green
833	③	203	Golden Yellow
730	⑧	34	Dark Yellow Green
640	⊞	215	Earth Color
368	⊞	224	Verdigris Green
368	⊞	224	Verdigris Green; half cross-stitch
321	⊟	97	Bright Red
321	⊠	97	Bright Red; three-quarter cross-stitch
321	⊡	97	Bright Red; backstitch
892	⊠	86	Fresh Red
892	⊡	86	Fresh Red; three-quarter cross-stitch
320	⊠	10	Fresh Green
986	⊠	30	Dark Green
986	⊡	30	Dark Green; half cross-stitch
986	⌐	30	Dark Green; backstitch

CROWBERRY

DMC		DANISH	
823	L	201	Dark Blue
310	✹	240	Black
793	T	21	Light Blue
436	Z	213	Medium Brown
833	3	203	Golden Yellow
640	H	215	Earth Color
640	H	215	Earth Color; half cross-stitch
320	X	10	Fresh Green
3347	c	40	Fresh Pale Green
986	❧	30	Dark Green

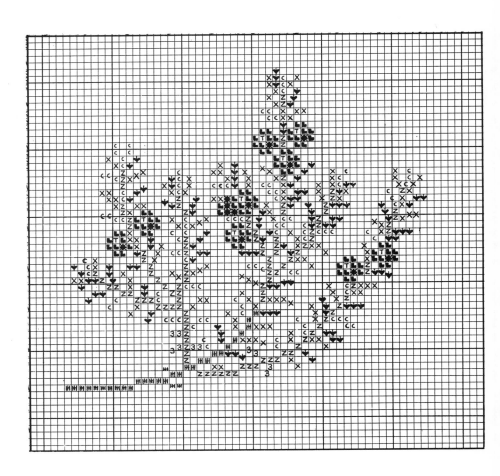

COWBERRY

DMC		DANISH	
500	▣	210	Deep Dark Green
986	❧	30	Dark Green
987	Q	100	Medium Green
640	H	215	Earth Color
921	↓	95	Carrot Color
892	Y	86	Fresh Red
730	8	34	Dark Yellow Green
730	⌐	34	Dark Yellow Green; backstitch
315	A	4	Wine Red
315	⌐	4	Wine Red; backstitch
3348	Z	223	Dull Light Green
3348	⋰	223	Dull Light Green; backstitch
320	X	10	Fresh Green
353	⊡	12	Light Brick Red

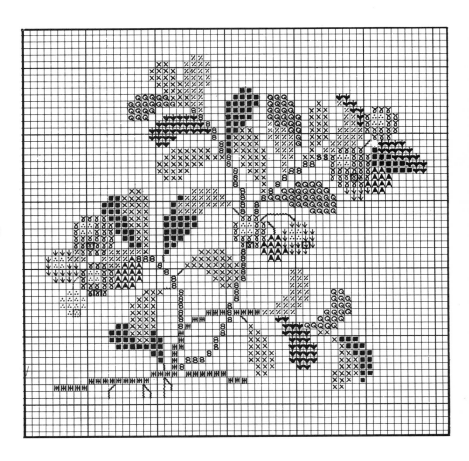

CLOUDBERRY

DMC		DANISH	
745	Ⓛ	16	Pale Light Yellow
741	◌	53	Orange Yellow
921	↓	95	Carrot Color
986	▼	30	Dark Green
407	Ⓗ	15	Greyish Red
315	Ⓐ	4	Wine Red
892	⊠	86	Fresh Red
892	⌐	86	Fresh Red; backstitch
320	⊠	10	Fresh Green
3347	Ⓒ	40	Fresh Pale Green
730	⑧	34	Dark Yellow Green

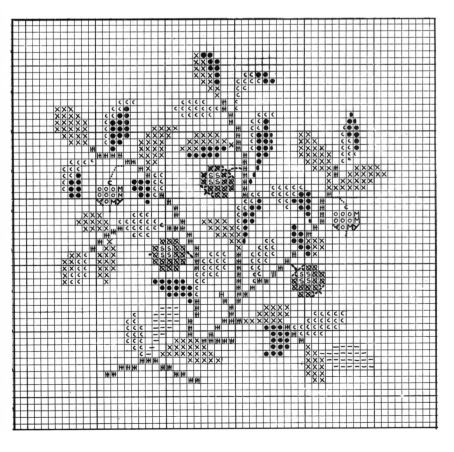

BILBERRY

DMC		DANISH	
414	Ⓢ	20	Grey
640	⒣	215	Earth Color
677	⊟	225	Light Yellow Green
3347	Ⓒ	40	Fresh Pale Green
3347	⌐	40	Fresh Pale Green; half cross-stitch
3347	⋮	40	Fresh Pale Green; backstitch
501	●	9	Dull Blue Green
501	▣	9	Dull Blue Green; half cross-stitch
309	Ⓜ	88	Bluish Red
309	◩	88	Bluish Red; three-quarter cross-stitch
961	Ⓞ	37	Fresh Bluish Red
961	▨	37	Fresh Bluish Red; three-quarter cross-stitch
550	⊠	23	Lavender
550	▧	23	Lavender; three-quarter cross-stitch
550	◹	23	Lavender; backstitch
320	⊠	10	Fresh Green

LESSER CRANE'S BILL

DMC		DANISH	
309	Ⓜ	88	Bluish Red
315	▲	4	Wine Red
3348	▨	223	Dull Light Green
986	▼	30	Dark Green
986	▣	30	Dark Green; half cross-stitch
500	◼	210	Very Dark Green
320	⊠	10	Fresh Green
320	Ꮑ	10	Fresh Green; backstitch

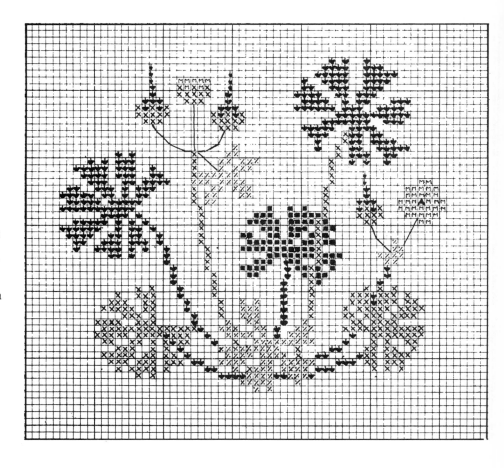

PANSIES

DMC		DANISH	
677	⊟	225	Light Yellow Green
3021	▲	216	Very Dark Brown
501	◉	9	Dull Blue Green
501	Ꮑ	9	Dull Blue Green; backstitch
791	▨	202	Navy Blue
793	Ⓣ	21	Light Blue
3348	▨	223	Dull Light Green
445	▨	31	Lemon Yellow

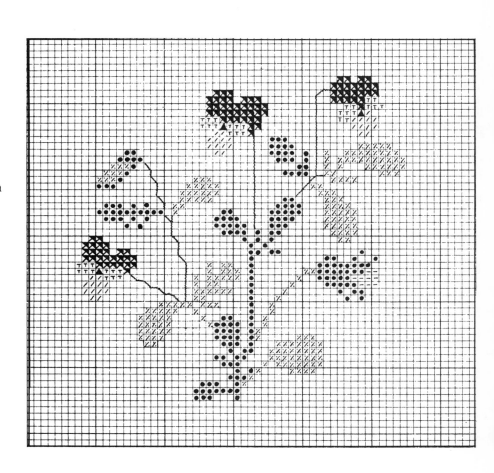

COWSLIP

DMC		DANISH	
320	⊠	10	Fresh Green
320	⊠	10	Fresh Green; three-quarter cross-stitch
501	◉	9	Dull Blue Green
912	⊠	8	Dark Verdigris Green
3348	⊠	223	Dull Light Green
3347	⊂	40	Fresh Pale Green
677	⊟	225	Light Yellow Green
745	⊔	16	Pale Light Yellow
445	⊘	31	Lemon Yellow
407	⊞	15	Greyish Red

CAT'S-FOOT

DMC		DANISH	
368	⊞	224	Verdigris Green
912	⊠	8	Dark Verdigris Green
3348	⊠	223	Dull Light Green
987	⊘	100	Medium Green
436	⊠	213	Medium Brown
320	⊠	10	Fresh Green
640	⊞	215	Earth Color
353	⊡	12	Light Brick Red
309	Ⓜ	88	Bluish Red
	⊡	0	White

GROUND IVY

DMC		DANISH	
320	⊠	10	Fresh Green
320	⌐	10	Fresh Green; backstitch
987	◙	100	Medium Green
987	⌐	100	Medium Green; backstitch
833	③	203	Golden Yellow
833	⋰	203	Golden Yellow; backstitch
793	⊤	21	Light Blue
3348	☒	223	Dull Light Green
355	⸬	214	Brownish Red; backstitch

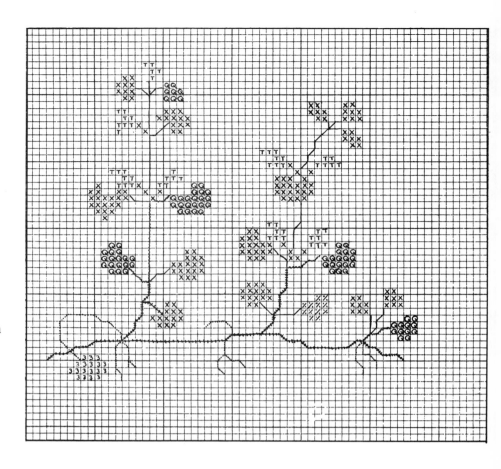

LADY'S-MANTLE

DMC		DANISH	
320	⊠	10	Fresh Green
501	◉	9	Dull Blue Green
501	⸬	9	Dull Blue Green; backstitch
734	⑤	26	Yellow Green
734	⋰	26	Yellow Green; backstitch
640	⋈	215	Earth Color
640	⌐	215	Earth Color; backstitch
3348	☒	223	Dull Light Green
677	⊟	225	Light Yellow Green

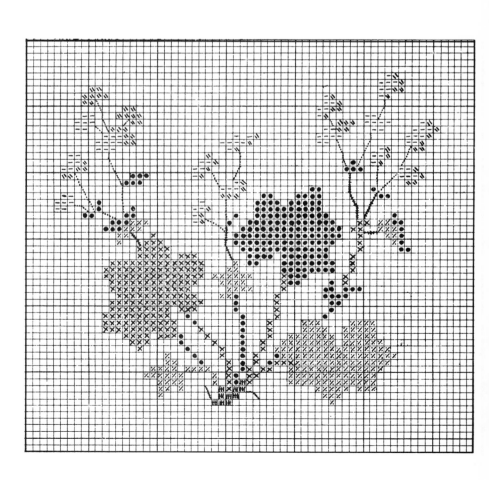

FIELD SCABIOUS REPEAT PATTERN

DMC		DANISH	
961	⊘	37	Fresh Bluish Red
961		37	Fresh Bluish Red; half cross-stitch
730	⊠	34	Dark Yellow Green
730		34	Dark Yellow Green; half cross-stitch
3021	◢◣	216	Very Dark Brown; backstitch
677	⚀⚀	225	Light Yellow Green; backstitch

NOTE: The diagram within the dotted line is the repeat.

BLACK CURRANTS
REPEAT PATTERN

DMC		DANISH	
309	M	88	Bluish Red
778	⊡	1	Pale Rose
3354	◁	3	Old Rose
315	◫	94	Dark Blue Violet
414	S	20	Grey
823	◣	201	Dark Blue
501	◙	9	Dull Blue Green
320	⊠	10	Fresh Green
987	◕	100	Medium Green
3348	⊘	223	Dull Light Green
500	◙	210	Very Dark Green
677	⊟	225	Light Yellow Green
3347	c	40	Fresh Pale Green
640	⊞	215	Earth Color
407	⌐	15	Greyish Red; backstitch

NOTE: The repeat extends between the two dotted lines on the chart.

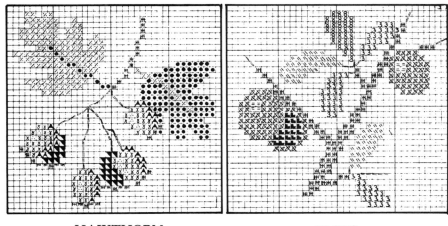

HAWTHORN   SLOES

WILD FRUIT

DMC		DANISH	
320	⊠	10	Fresh Green
320	⌐	10	Fresh Green; backstitch
501	◉	9	Dull Blue Green
501	⅏	9	Dull Blue Green; backstitch
400	◣	29	Dark Brownish Red
315	▲	4	Wine Red
833	③	203	Golden Yellow
734	◩	26	Yellow Green
3348	▨	223	Dull Light Green
3348	⠤	223	Dull Light Green; backstitch
730	▣	34	Dark Yellow Green
730	⠇	34	Dark Yellow Green; backstitch
321	⊟	97	Bright Red
892	⊠	86	Fresh Red
444	⅄	48	Yellow
677	⊟	225	Light Yellow Green
550	⊠	23	Lavender
318	⊟	19	Pale Grey
823	◪	201	Dark Blue
327	⊡	5	Lilac
407	⊞	15	Greyish Red
640	⊞	215	Earth Color
640	⊞	215	Earth Color; half cross-stitch
640	⌐	215	Earth Color; backstitch
353	⊡	12	Light Brick Red

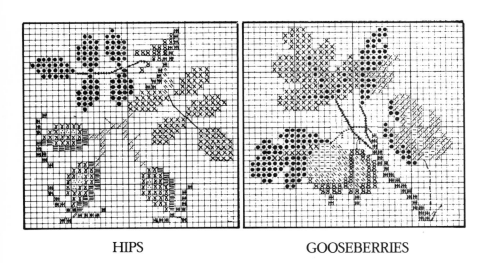

HIPS   GOOSEBERRIES

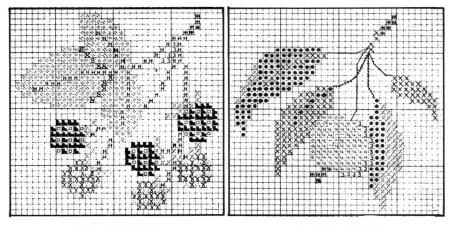

BRAMBLES   CRABAPPLES

SIX STRAND EMBROIDERY COTTON (FLOSS) CONVERSION CHART

KEY: T = Possible Substitute   * = Close Match   — = No Match

DMC NO.	ROYAL MOULINÉ NO.	BATES/ANCHOR NO.
White	1001	2
Ecru	8600	926
208	3335*	110*
209	3415*	105
210	3320*	104
211	3410	108*
221	2570	897*
223	2555	894
224	2545	893
225	2540	892
300	8330	352*
301	8315*	349*
304	2415*	47*
307	6005*	289*
309	2525*	42*
310	1002	403
311	4275T	149*
312	—	147*
315	3130	896*
316	3120	895*
317	1030*	400*
318	1020*	399*
319	5025	246*
320	5015	216*
321	2415	47
322	—	978*
326	2530*	59*
327	3365*	101*
333	—	119
334	4250T	145
335	2525T	42*
336	4270*	149*
340	—	118
341	—	117
347	2425*	13*
349	2400	13
350	2045T	11
351	2015T	11*
352	2015	10*
353	2010*	8*
355	8095	5968
356	8090	5975*
367	5020	216*
368	5005*	240*
369	5005	213*
370	—	889*
371	—	888*
372	2400	887*
400	8325*	351
402	8305*	347*
407	8005*	882*
413	1025*	401
414	1020*	400*
415	1015	398
420	8720*	375*
422	8710*	373*
433	8265	371*
434	8215	309
435	8210*	369*
436	8205	363*

DMC NO.	ROYAL MOULINÉ NO.	BATES/ANCHOR NO.
437	8200*	362
444	6155*	291
445	6000	288
451	—	399*
452	1015T	399*
453	5255	397*
469	5255	267*
470	5255*	267
471	5245	266*
472	5240	264*
498	2425T	20*
500	5125	879*
501	5120*	878
502	5110	876
503	5105	875
504	5100	213*
517	—	169*
518	4860*	168*
519	4855T	167*
520	—	862*
522	—	859*
523	—	859*
524	1115T	858*
535	—	401*
543	8500	933*
550	3380*	102*
552	3370*	101
553	3360	98
554	3355*	96*
561	—	212*
562	—	210*
563	—	208*
564	—	203*
580	5935	267*
581	5925	266*
597	4860*	168*
598	4855*	167*
600	2225*	59*
601	2225*	78*
602	2640*	77*
603	2720*	76*
604	2710	75*
605	2155	50*
606	7260	335
608	7255	333*
610	5825T	889*
611	5735T	898
612	8815*	832
613	5605*	956*
632	8530	936*
640	8625	903
642	8620*	392
644	8800	830
645	1115	905*
646	1115*	8581*
647	1110	8581
648	1100*	900
666	2405	46
676	6250	891
677	—	886*

DMC NO.	ROYAL MOULINÉ NO.	BATES/ANCHOR NO.
680	6260*	901
699	5375	923*
700	5365*	229
701	5365*	227
702	5330	239
703	5320	238
704	5310*	256*
712	8600*	387*
718	3015*	88
720	—	326
721	—	324*
722	—	323*
725	6215	306*
726	6150*	295
727	6135	293
729	6255	890
730	—	924*
731	—	281*
732	5925T	281*
733	—	280*
734	—	279*
738	8245*	942
739	8240*	885*
740	7045	316
741	6125	304
742	6120	303
743	6210	297
744	6110*	301*
745	6105	300*
746	6100	386*
747	4850	158*
754	8075	778*
758	8080	868
760	2035	9*
761	2030	8*
762	1010*	397
772	—	264*
775	4600*	128*
776	2110*	24*
778	3110	968*
780	8215*	310*
781	8215	309*
782	6230	308*
783	6220*	307
791	4165*	941*
792	4155T	940
793	4155	121
794	4145	120*
796	4340	133*
797	4265*	132*
798	4325	131*
799	4250*	130*
800	4310	128
801	8405	357*
806	4870T	169*
807	4860*	168*
809	4145*	130*
813	4610*	160*
814	2340T	44*
815	2530*	43

DMC NO.	ROYAL MOULINÉ NO.	BATES/ANCHOR NO.
816	2530	44*
817	2415T	19
818	2505*	48
819	2000	892*
820	4345	134
822	8605*	387*
823	4400*	150
824	4225	164*
825	4215	162*
826	4210	161*
827	4605	159*
828	4850	158*
829	5825	906
830	5825*	889*
831	5825T	889*
832	5815	907
833	5815*	874*
834	5810*	874
838	8425*	380
839	8560	380*
840	8555	379*
841	8550	378*
842	8505	376*
844	1115T	401*
869	8720*	944*
890	5025*	879*
891	2135	35*
892	2130	28
893	2125*	27
894	2115T	26
895	5430*	246*
898	8425*	360
899	2515	27*
900	7230*	333
902	—	72*
904	5295*	258*
905	5295	258*
906	5285*	256*
907	5280*	255
909	5370	229*
910	5370*	228*
911	5465*	205*
912	5465	205
913	5460*	209
915	3030	89*
917	3020*	89*
918	8330*	341*
919	8095*	341*
920	8060*	339*
921	8060*	349*
922	8315T	324*
924	4830T	851*
926	4820*	779*
927	4810T	849*
928	1010T	900*
930	4510	922*
931	4505	921*
932	4500	920*
934	5070T	862*
935	5225T	862*

DMC NO.	ROYAL MOULINÉ NO.	BATES/ANCHOR NO.
936	5260T	269
937	5260	268
938	8430	381
939	4405	127
943	4935*	188*
945	8020*	347*
946	7230*	332*
947	7255*	330*
948	8070	778*
950	8020T	4146
951	8020T	366*
954	5455*	203*
955	5450	206*
956	2170*	40*
957	2160T	40*
958	—	187
959	—	186
961	2515*	76*
962	2515	76*
963	2505	49*
964	5150*	185
966	7040	214*
970	7045	316*
971	7045	316*
972	6120*	298
973	6015	290
975	8365	355*
976	8355	308*
977	8350	307*
986	5430	246*
987	5020T	244*
988	5295T	243*
989	5405T	242*
991	5165T	189*
992	4925*	187*
993	4915*	186*
995	4710	410
996	4700	433
3011	5525T	845*
3012	5525*	844*
3013	5810	842*
3021	5515	382*
3022	—	8581*
3023	—	8581*
3024	1100	900*
3031	8620T	905*
3032	8620T	903*
3033	8610*	388*
3041	3215*	871
3042	3205*	869
3045	6260T	373*
3046	5810	887*
3047	5805	886*
3051	5530T	846*
3052	5060*	859*
3053	5055*	859*
3064	8005*	914*
3072	4805*	920*
3078	6130	292*
3325	4200	159*

DMC NO.	ROYAL MOULINÉ NO.	BATES/ANCHOR NO.
3326	2115*	25*
3328	2045	11*
3340	—	329
3341	—	328
3345	5025T	268*
3346	5220T	257*
3347	5210*	266*
3348	5270*	265
3350	2220	42*
3354	2210	74*
3362	—	862*
3363	—	861*
3364	—	843*
3371	8435	382
3607	—	87*
3608	—	86
3609	—	85
3685	2335	70*
3687	2325	69*
3688	2320	66*
3689	2310	49
3705	—	35*
3706	—	28*
3708	—	26*
48	9000*	1201*
51	9014	1220
52	9006	1208
53	—	—
57	9002	1203
61	9013T	1201*
62	9000T	1201*
67	—	1211*
69	9002	1218*
75	9002	1206*
90	9012T	1217*
91	9008*	1211
92	9011T	1216*
93	9007*	1210*
94	9011*	1216
95	9006T	1208*
99	9005T	1207*
101	9009*	1213*
102	—	1208*
103	—	1210*
104	9012	1217
105	9013*	1218
106	9002T	1203*
107	9003	1204
108	9014*	1220*
111	—	1218*
112	9003T	1204*
113	9007*	1210*
114	9010	1215
115	9004	1206
121	9007	1210
122	9010T	1215*
123	—	1213*
124	9007T	1210*
125	9009	1213
126	9006*	1208*